Black
Achievement
IN SCIENCE

Inventors

Mason Crest

Black
Achievement
IN SCIENCE

Biology

Chemistry

Computer Science

Engineering

Environmental Science

Inventors

Medicine

Physics

Space

Technology

Black
Achievement
IN SCIENCE

Inventors

By MARI RICH
Foreword by Malinda Gilmore and Mel Poulson,
National Organization for the Advancement of
Black Chemists and Chemical Engineers

Mason Crest
450 Parkway Drive, Suite D
Broomall, PA 19008
www.masoncrest.com

Series ISBN: 978-1-4222-3554-6
Hardback ISBN: 978-1-4222-3560-7
EBook ISBN: 978-1-4222-8327-1

First printing
1 3 5 7 9 8 6 4 2

Produced by Shoreline Publishing Group LLC
Santa Barbara, California
Editorial Director: James Buckley Jr.
Designer: Patty Kelley
Production: Sandy Gordon
www.shorelinepublishing.com
Cover photograph by Chris Hamilton.

Library of Congress Cataloging-in-Publication Data

Names: Rich, Mari.
Title: Inventors / by Mari Rich ; foreword by Malinda Gilmore, Ph.D., Executive Board Chair, and Mel
    Poulson, Executive Board Vice-Chair, National Organization for the Professional Advancement of Black
    Chemists and Chemical Engineers (NOBCChE).
Description: Broomall, PA : Mason Crest, [2017] | Series: Black achievement in science | Includes index.
    Identifiers: LCCN 2016002448 | ISBN 9781422235607 (hardback) | ISBN 9781422235546 (series) | ISBN
    9781422283271 (ebook)
Subjects: LCSH: Inventors--United States--Biography--Juvenile literature. | African American inventors--
    Biography--Juvenile literature.
Classification: LCC T39 .R47 2017 | DDC 609.2/396073--dc23
LC record available at http://lccn.loc.gov/2016002448

Key Icons to Look for

 Words to Understand: These words with their easy-to-understand definitions will increase the reader's understanding of the text, while building vocabulary skills.

 Research Projects: Readers are pointed toward areas of further inquiry connected to each chapter. Suggestions are provided for projects that encourage deeper research and analysis.

 Text-Dependent Questions: These questions send the reader back to the text for more careful attention to the evidence presented here.

 Series Glossary of Key Terms: This back-of-the-book glossary contains terminology used throughout this series. Words found here increase the reader's ability to read and comprehend higher-level books and articles in this field.

 Educational Videos: Readers can view videos by scanning our QR codes, providing them with additional educational content to supplement the text. Examples include news coverage, moments in history, speeches, iconic moments, and much more!

cience, Technology, Engineering and Mathematics (STEM) are vital to our future, the future of our country, the future of our regions, and the future of our children. STEM is everywhere and it shapes our everyday experiences. Science and technology have become the leading foundation of global development. Both subjects continue to improve the quality of life as new findings, inventions, and creations emerge from the basis of science. A career in a STEM discipline is a fantastic choice and one that should be explored by many.

In today's society, STEM is becoming more diverse and even internationalized. However, the shortage of African Americans and other minorities, including women, still exists. This series—***Black Achievement in Science***—reveals the numerous career choices and pathways that great African-American scientists, technologists, engineers, and mathematicians have pursued to become successful in a STEM discipline. The purpose of this series of books is to inspire, motivate, encourage, and educate people about the numerous career choices and pathways in STEM. We applaud the authors for sharing the experiences of our forefathers and foremothers and ultimately increasing the number of people of color in STEM and, more

By Malinda Gilmore, NOBCChE Executive Board Chair and Mel Poulson, NOBCChE Executive Board Vice-Chair specifically, increasing the number of African Americans to pursue careers in STEM.

The personal experiences and accomplishments shared within are truly inspiring and gratifying. It is our hope that by reading about the lives and careers of these great scientists, technologists, engineers, and mathematicians, the reader might become inspired and totally committed to pursue a career in a STEM discipline and say to themselves, "If they were able to do it, then I am definitely able to do it, and this, too, can be me." Hopefully, the reader will realize that these great accomplishments didn't come easily. It was because of hard work, perseverance, and determination that these chosen individuals were so successful.

As Executive Board Members of The National Organization for the Professional Advancement of Black Chemists and Chemical Engineers (NOBCChE) we are excited about this series. For more than 40 years, NOBCChE has promoted the STEM fields and its mission is to build an eminent cadre of people of color in STEM. Our mission is in line with the overall purpose of this series and we are indeed committed to inspiring our youth to explore and contribute to our country's future in science, technology, engineering, and mathematics.

We encourage all readers to enjoy the series in its entirety and identify with a personal story that resonates well with you. Learn more about that person and their career pathway, and you can be just like them.

The creativity of inventors created this chip, now used in other inventions.

ike every other group of people, black people have been inventing ways to make life easier, safer, and generally better for a very long time. Just within the last century-and-a-half, black inventors created devices that made it possible for ordinary middle-class people to buy affordable shoes (Jan Matzeliger, who devised an automatic shoe-lasting machine); more efficient to manufacture electric light bulbs (Lewis Latimer, an associate and sometimes rival of Thomas Edison); easier to defend ourselves (Andre Reboucas, who conceived the idea of the underwater torpedo); and more safely feed our families (Lloyd Hall, who transformed the food-preservation industry). In more recent decades, black inventors have revolutionized the computer industry (Mark Dean), helped NASA bring satellite images back from space (Valerie Thomas), and had a hand in the development of Silicon Valley (Roy Clay). The list is endless: There are very few areas in which black inventors have not made a mark.

Before the Emancipation Proclamation was signed in 1863, however, it was sometimes unusual for African-American inventors to get credit for their work. Slaves were totally prohibited from filing for a patent, so their unscrupulous owners profited instead, and even free blacks who were able to obtain patents were often not well compensated or celebrated (such as Thomas Jennings, a tailor from New York, who was awarded a patent in 1821 for a dry-cleaning process—the first instance of an African-American inventor being acknowledged by the US Patent Office).

That situation changed somewhat thanks to the work of Henry E. Baker, a former Navy midshipman who later attended law school and went on to become Second Assistant Examiner at the Patent Office.

Baker discovered some 1,200 African-American inventors, and about two-thirds of those gave permission for him to reveal their identities. (Such were the times that the other third feared that if consumers knew they were black, sales of their inventions would either decline sharply or stop altogether.)

It is thanks in large part to Baker's efforts that we know of the early inventors discussed in this volume, who did a great deal to, as he wrote, "multiply human comforts and minimize human misery" despite racism, lack of funds, and other formidable challenges.

The world has come a long way since early Stone Age inventors created the first tools, but there are still plenty of comforts to be multiplied and miseries to be minimized.

In the final chapter, find out more about what it takes to come up with an invention. ●

Words to Understand

abolitionist
a person who supported the unconditional and immediate ending of slavery in the US (considered an exceptionally radical idea before the Civil War)

celestial
having to do with space or the heavens

gristmill
a mill for grinding grain

hyperbole
exaggeration

pension
money paid to retirees

Quaker
a member of the Religious Society of Friends; the Quakers are a group of Christians who believe in living and worshipping simply and who are known for their devotion to pacifism and social justice

Benjamin Banneker

Born:
1731

Died:
1806

Nationality:
American

Achievements:
Creative inventor and
watchmaker who defied
the odds to succeed
in a divided time

Benjamin Banneker is a somewhat divisive figure among historians. Many hail him as one of the most important African-American inventors who ever lived, as well as a pioneering astronomer, mathematician, and statesman; others assert that his achievements have become exaggerated over time or that some accomplishments have been falsely attributed to him.

Historians have not reached consensus even on Banneker's ancestry. It is known that he was born on November 9, 1731, in Baltimore County, Maryland. His mother, Mary, had been born into freedom, and his father, Robert, was a freed slave who had been brought to the U.S. from Guinea. Although some early sources assert that there are no white ancestors in Banneker's family tree, later biographers believe that his maternal

grandmother was a Caucasian indentured servant named Molly Walsh, who somehow purchased and married an African slave named Banneka, in defiance of Maryland law.

Molly, who reportedly taught Banneker to read, established a 100-acre farm in Baltimore's Patapsco River Valley. Baltimore County was then home to some 200 free blacks, along with 4,000 slaves and 13,000 whites. As a youth, Banneker, who had three sisters, met Peter Heinrichs, a **Quaker** teacher who established a small school near the farm. Heinrichs, like all Quakers, was a staunch **abolitionist** and believer in equality for everyone. He loaned Banneker books and arranged for him to attend classes—a happy state of affairs that continued until Banneker was needed to help work on the farm. Heinrichs was just the first of Banneker's Caucasian mentors, and biographers who question the inventor's accomplishments sometimes point out that those early supporters had a deep emotional investment in touting his brilliance, sometimes to the point of **hyperbole**.

When Banneker was in his early 20s, he became fascinated by a pocket watch owned by a family friend, Josef Levi. Delighted by the young man's intellectual curiosity, Levi gave Banneker the timepiece as a gift. Banneker repeatedly disassembled the watch and then put it back together to teach himself how it worked. He hit upon the idea of building a larger version and began borrowing books on geometry and the laws of motion. It took two years of planning (calculating the proper number of teeth for each gear and the necessary spacing between the gears) and build-

A gristmill uses the power of flowing water to turn a wheel that causes gears to rotate, crushing wheat into flour.

ing (carving each needed piece meticulously by hand), but in 1753 he finally completed the project. His clock, which struck on the hour, kept perfect time for more than five decades and is widely acknowledged as the first clock ever made entirely in the US.

Banneker's next set of invention adventures began when he became friendly with the Ellicott brothers, part of a Quaker family who built a series of **gristmills** in Baltimore County in the 1770s. In 1788, using tools and books he had borrowed from the Ellicotts, Banneker tried predicting the timing of a solar eclipse. While he was slightly off in his calculations, he found later that the error was due to a mistake in something he had read rather than an actual miscalculation on his part.

In early 1791, Banneker helped another member of that family, Major Andrew Ellicott, to survey the new federal city that would become Washington, D.C. The new capi-

tal was to be established on land along the Potomac River that Maryland and Virginia had given to the federal government; the territory was in the shape of a square measuring 10 miles on each side. Ellicott's team placed boundary stones at mile points along the borders, and Banneker's major contribution was to make astronomical observations at Jones Point in Alexandria, to determine the exact starting point for the survey.

Aside from his clock, Banneker is perhaps most widely celebrated for his interactions with Thomas Jefferson, and some sources even credit the inventor with penning the first protest letter on record. Enclosing a copy of an almanac he had compiled, in mid-1791 Banneker wrote Secretary of State Jefferson a lengthy, unflinching letter in which he referenced the Declaration of Independence.

Jefferson's response was polite but he did not praise the almanac and years later he told a friend that Banneker had obviously had a great deal

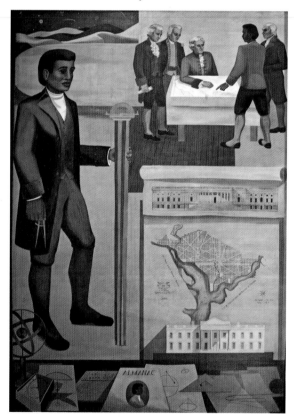

A mural in Washington D.C. by artist Maxime Seelbinder celebrates Banneker's deeds.

of help in compiling the book. In 1792, a few months after showing it to Jefferson, Banneker published that first almanac, creating an ephemeris (a table of the position of **celestial** bodies), and including information about the tides, political commentary, excerpts from literature, and other items of interest. The public was much more appreciative than the secretary of state and future president, and Banneker ultimately published six volumes.

Banneker gradually sold off most of his family land and then gave the rest to the Ellicott family in exchange for a small **pension**. He died on October 9, 1806, and his obituary stated: "Mr. Banneker is a prominent instance to prove that a descendant of Africa is susceptible of as great mental improvement and deep knowledge into the mysteries of nature as that of any other nation."

On the day of his funeral, the small log cabin in which Banneker had been living caught on fire. His papers and possessions, including his clock, which still kept perfect time, were destroyed in the blaze. ●

Benjamin Banneker:
Inventor in the Early Colonies

Words to Understand

affluent
wealthy, well-off

precursor
something that comes before something else and that often leads to or influences its development

subterfuge
the use of tricks to hide, avoid, or get something

Garrett Morgan

Born:
1877

Died:
1963

Nationality:
American

Achievements:
Invented three-color
stoplight, early gas mask,
and safety cigarettes

Amassing a list of inventions as long as that of Garrett Morgan would be an impressive achievement for anyone. He is responsible for the world's first three-light traffic signal and for the **precursor** to the modern gas mask, among other important innovations. His accomplishments seem all the more noteworthy, however, considering that Garrett was the son of a former slave and had only an elementary-school education.

Garrett Augustus Morgan, Sr., was born on March 4, 1877 in Claysville, a black community in Kentucky. His father was reportedly both the slave and offspring of John H. Morgan, a Confederate colonel. Garrett's mother was the former Eliza Reed, who was said to be part Native American.

Morgan, the seventh of the 11 children born to the couple, attended school until the

sixth grade before dropping out to help his family financial-ly. As a teen, he moved to Cincinnati, Ohio, hoping to earn a good living there. Initially, he took a job as a handyman for an **affluent** landowner, and he saved part of his wages to hire a private tutor in an effort to better himself.

In 1895, Morgan moved to Cleveland, where he was hired by the owner of a textile business to repair sewing machines. There he invented his first device: a belt fastener that increased the efficiency of the machines. In 1907, he struck out on his own, opening a sewing machine shop, and a few years later he launched a women's clothing store that boasted more than 30 employees.

One day, Morgan noticed that the needles on his sewing machines moved so quickly that they left scorch marks on the fabric. He began experimenting with a chemical solu-tion that he thought might reduce the friction between the needle and the cloth and realized that as a side effect, the cloth's fibers became straighter. Excited by the possibilities, he applied the solution to a stray dog, whose fur became demonstrably smoother and less kinked. When the product worked equally well on his own hair, he launched the G.A. Morgan Hair Refining Company and marketed it to African Americans. (He later added hair dye and a straightening comb to his line.)

The revenue the new firm generated allowed Morgan to pursue his passion for inventing. He got his next big idea while watching firefighters extinguishing a blaze and struggling to breathe in the midst of the smoke. His hood-like device, now widely acknowledged as the precursor to the modern gas mask, featured a wet sponge to filter out the smoke and cool the air. An intake tube hung from the hood to the floor, allowing in fresh, breathable air. Since smoke and heat rise, the air at the bottom of a burning room is cleaner and cooler. Morgan filed for a patent in 1912, and two years later, after the device had won a medal at the International Exposition of Sanitation and Safety, he founded the National Safety Device Company to market it.

Because of the racism of the era, it was not always easy to make sales, and Morgan sometimes resorted to the **subterfuge** of hiring a white actor to pretend to be the product's inventor. Sometimes he represented himself as a Native American chief and demonstrated the hood by building a fire fueled by tar, sulfur, and manure within a closed tent and remaining inside for several minutes before emerging, unaffected by the smoke.

In 1916, Morgan got a chance to demonstrate his

This is a recreation of the safety hood Morgan invented.

hood in a real-life situation, when a tunnel exploded under Lake Erie. Multiple rescue attempts had failed as the rescuers themselves succumbed to the smoke. When word of the incident reached him in the middle of the night, Morgan, still wearing his pajamas, raced to the scene with his brother. The pair dashed into the tunnel and retrieved two victims, and when others at the scene witnessed their success, they quickly donned the extra hoods Morgan had brought with him and saved additional men. Although Morgan himself ultimately made four trips into the tunnel, his contributions were ignored by city officials and the media until several years later. (The International Association of Fire Engineers, however, made him an honorary member.)

Morgan was the first black man in Cleveland to own an automobile, and when he witnessed a serious accident at an intersection one day, he began to think of ways to make driving less dangerous. Although traffic lights had first been installed in London, England, years before, they had only two signals, for "stop" and "go." Morgan correctly reasoned that a third signal—indicating that drivers coming from all

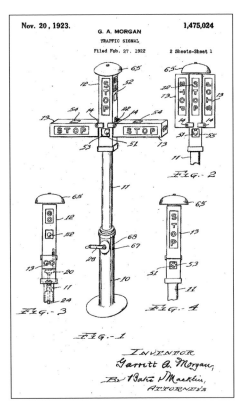

This shows part of the patent application drawing for the traffic light.

directions should stop to allow pedestrians to cross—would regulate traffic in a more orderly, safer manner. In 1923, the US Patent Office granted him Patent No. 1,475,024 for the hand-operated signal, and he later sold the rights to General Electric for $40,000. Morgan's invention was deployed throughout the country until all manual traffic signals were replaced by the automatic red, yellow, and green light devices currently in widespread use.

Morgan, who helped found the Cleveland Association of Colored Men and was active in numerous other civic groups, developed glaucoma in the mid-1940s and ultimately lost his vision. He died on August 27, 1963. In Cleveland, there is now a street named after him, as well as a science-focused high school. He continued to tinker until the end of his life, and among his final inventions was a self-extinguishing cigarette, which featured a tiny water-filled sac near the filter. ●

Garrett Morgan:
Inventions made us safer

Words to Understand

boiler
a large device in which boiling water creates steam heat in buildings

rectory
residence of a priest or minister

Frederick McKinley Jones

Born:
1893

Died:
1991

Nationality:
American

Achievements:
Revolutionized grocery
industry by creating
refrigerated trucks
and storage

When Frederick McKinley Jones got the idea for a refrigerator unit that could be used in long-haul trucks and train cars, he revolutionized the grocery industry. The work he did enabled the creation of the frozen-food business, made it possible for fresh meat and produce to be delivered over far-flung areas, and changed the eating habits of the entire nation.

Jones was born in Cincinnati, Ohio, on May 17, 1893, to an African-American mother and an Irish father. Some mythology surrounds his early years. Most sources agree that by the age of nine he was being raised by a minister in Covington, Kentucky. While some say that both his parents were deceased, others suggest that only his mother had died and that his overwhelmed father had sent him to live with the priest because no local orphanages would take in black children.

As a young man, Jones put his mechanical skills to work on race cars similar to this one being used in a modern race.

Various sources claim that Jones—who cooked, cleaned, and gardened to earn his keep at the **rectory**—left the priest's care at either age 11 or age 16 to make his own way in the world, and there is also disagreement as to whether he stopped attending school in the sixth or eighth grade.

It is known that at some point he returned to Cincinnati and found work as an assistant at the R.C. Crothers Garage. He had always shown a skill for mechanics—he enjoyed tinkering with the parishioners' cars when they parked at the rectory, fixing minor problems—and within a few years he had been promoted to shop foreman. In his late teens Jones began building and racing his own cars, and he was soon a well-known figure on the Great Lakes region's racing scene.

Jones worked for a time as a handyman at a local hotel, and one day in about 1912 a guest, impressed by his skill in repairing a **boiler**, invited him to move to a 50,000-acre family farm in Hallock, Minnesota. There he put Jones in charge of maintaining all of the cars and farm machinery on the property.

Drafted during World War I, Jones served in France as an electrician, and he earned high praise for wiring army camps for electricity, telephone, and telegraph service. Known for his ability to fix anything, he was also sent to the frontlines to repair military vehicles, portable X-ray machines, and communications equipment, and he ultimately achieved the rank of sergeant, a rare honor for a black soldier at that time.

In 1919, Jones was discharged from the military and returned to Hallock, which he had grown to love. He once told an interviewer that the town was a place where a person was "judged more on his character and ability than on the color of his skin." Jones resumed racing but abandoned that hobby after he crashed a car on a particularly sharp curve. He kept busy in other ways, however. He began taking a correspondence course in electrical engineering and once built a transmitter for a local radio station. He also attached skis to an old airplane body, added a motor, and used the improvised vehicle to ferry his neighbors around town when the snow was heavy. Among his clients were several local doctors, and at their suggestion, Jones created a portable X-ray machine that could be taken on house calls. Although the device worked well, he neglected to apply for a patent and never earned a profit for his work.

In 1927, Joseph A. Numero, a Minneapolis businessman who made projectors and other machinery used in movie

theaters, heard of Jones's skills and hired him to make improvements in some of the products. Jones converted the silent-movie projectors so they could play films with sound; devised ways to improve the picture quality; and invented an automatic ticket-dispensing machine, which he patented in 1939.

One day, when a friend of Numero's was complaining about how hard it was for someone in the grocery business to ship perishable food, Jones hit upon the idea of inventing a refrigeration unit that could keep a truck cool while withstanding the bumps of the road. He patented the device

Refrigerated trucks are now seen all around the world, delivering food and other perishables safely.

in 1940, and Numero, understanding its potential to change the entire food industry, sold his cinema-supply company and entered into a partnership with Jones. By the end of the decade, the firm, which they called Thermo King, had made them an estimated $3 million, and its product line included refrigeration units not only for trucks but for trains and ships as well.

During World War II, Jones—who was the first black man ever to be elected to membership in the American Society of Refrigeration Engineers—developed an air-conditioning unit for military field hospitals and portable field refrigerators for storing blood and serum needed for transfusions. In the 1950s he served as a consultant for various branches of the U.S. government, including the Department of Defense and the Bureau of Standards.

Jones was awarded more than 60 patents during his lifetime. He died of lung cancer on February 21, 1961, and 3 years later, in 1991, President George H.W. Bush posthumously gave him the National Medal of Technology, making him the first African-American inventor ever to receive that prestigious honor. ●

Frederick Jones:
Refrigeration pioneer

Words to Understand

ambivalence
having mixed feelings about a topic

electret transducers
a material that remains permanently polarized after being subjected to a strong electrical field

transducer
a device that converts variations in a physical quantity, such as pressure or brightness, into an electrical signal

ubiquitous
available everywhere

James West

Born:
1931

Nationality:
American

Achievements:
Inventor of key parts of
modern microphones

James Edward Maceo West is a natural-born scientist. "Discovery is the best high I've ever had," he once told a journalist."It's extremely euphoric. It's true that there is very little new in nature, but we can discover more and more about nature." His greatest discovery came when he was working in the Acoustics Research Department at Bell Laboratories. His invention of **electret transducers** changed an entire industry, and his technology is still in use today in the vast majority of products containing microphones, including hearing aids (a development that gives him great pride) and military communications systems (about which he feels some **ambivalence**).

West was born on February 10, 1931, in Prince Edward County, Virginia. (The birth took place at home because his mother was

barred from the nearby whites-only hospital.) His father, Samuel, was an ambitious man who worked variously as a funeral home owner, insurance salesman, and railroad porter. His mother, Matilda, was a teacher who worked at Langley Air Force Base during World War II. At one point she lost her job because she was a member of the National Association for the Advancement of Colored People.

As a child, West loved to take things apart to see how they worked. He has quipped that no appliance was safe when he got a screwdriver and a pair of pliers. He had a cousin who worked part-time as a contractor, and when he was 12 years old, he helped install wiring in several rural Virginia homes that had never before had electricity.

As a youngster, West tinkered with electrical and radio parts.

The experience ignited his love of science, and he expressed interest in studying to be a chemist or physicist. His parents disapproved. "In those days in the South, the only professional jobs that seemed to be open to a black man were a teacher, a preacher, a doctor or a lawyer," he said during one interview. "My father introduced me to three black men who had earned doctorates in chemistry and physics. The

West earned a medal serving in the Army in the Korean War, which lasted from 1950 to 1953.

best jobs they could find were at the post office." An uncle had a small dental practice, and West's parents hoped that he, too, might become a dentist. (His only brother, Nathaniel, did become a dentist and ultimately went on to teach public-health dentistry at Howard University.)

West, trying to comply with their wishes, enrolled in the pre-med program at Virginia's Hampton University. When the Korean War broke out, West was drafted, and during his tour of duty, he was awarded a Purple Heart. Upon his return, he enrolled at Temple University, in Philadelphia, switching his major to physics. His parents, angered by his decision, cut off all financial support. West during this period, worked during the summers at Bell Laboratories, in Northern New Jersey, and after earning his B.S. degree in solid state physics in 1957, he was hired on a full-time basis.

There, he and a colleague, Gerhard Sessler, constructed a small microphone that did not require a battery, thanks to the use of electret technology. West had not previously heard of electrets, although he later found out that scientists had known of their existence for hundreds of years. "My life really changed at that point," he told an interviewer. "Understanding this phenomenon became the single purpose in my life. I made an effort to understand everything I could about electrets."

The electret microphone revolutionized communications technology, making other microphones virtually obsolete. The devices, smaller and more cost-effective than any other microphones on the market, were used in phones beginning in 1968, and they gradually became ubiquitous; today fully 90 percent of all products containing microphones make use of electrets. West was recognized for his

Without West's innovations, all these microphones would have trouble getting the job done!

accomplishments when, in 1999, he became only the fourth African-American figure elected to join the National Inventors Hall of Fame, and in 2006 he received the U.S. National Medal of Technology.

Although West—who began teaching at Johns Hopkins University in 2002—earned almost 50 US patents over the course of his career, he earned no money from them; researchers at Bell Laboratories were not allowed to personally profit from their own inventions. ●

James West:
Can you hear us now?

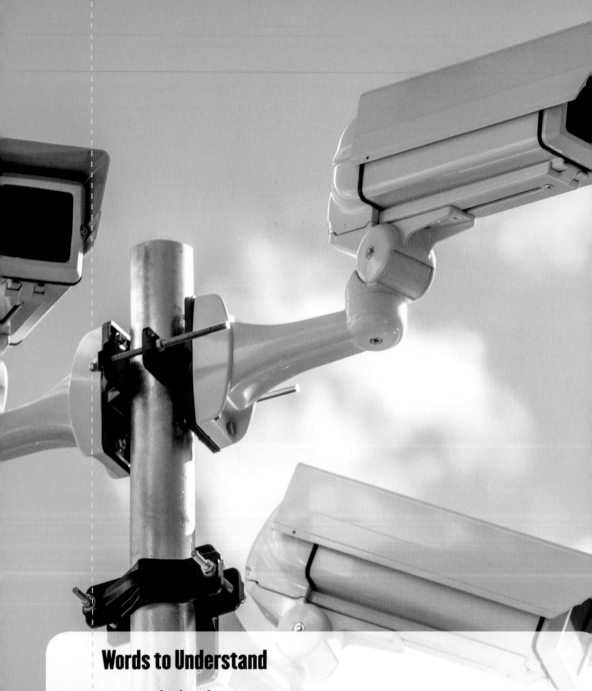

Words to Understand

predominantly
characterized as including a significant portion of one thing while in a group of many things

surveillance
the process of watching over people or a large area

Chapter 5

Marie Van Brittan Brown

Born:
1922

Died:
1999

Nationality:
American

Achievements:
Invented the first closed-circuit TV system, forerunner of today's modern security systems

According to market surveys, Americans now spend more than $20 billion on home security systems, and that number is expected to reach almost $35 billion within the next few years, as systems get increasingly more sophisticated and multifunctional.

The home security industry has undeniably come a long way since 1853, when Augustus Russell Pope was awarded a patent for a simple electromagnetic device that would ring a bell if a door or window was opened without authorization. A shrewd businessman named Edwin Holmes later bought the rights to the invention, marketing it to large corporate clients like Lord & Taylor and Tiffany's.

One of the most revolutionary innovations in home security systems came in the late 1960s with the introduction of closed cir-

cuit television **surveillance**, which allowed a property owner to actually view what was going on using a camera and screen. The inventor largely responsible for that innovation was a black woman: Marie Van Brittan Brown.

The future inventor was born Marie Felton Van Brittan on October 30, 1922, in the New York City borough of Queens. (According to some sources, her family hailed from St. Kitts, an island in the Caribbean.) Like many women of that era who found other professions closed to them, she became a nurse, and she often found herself caring for

Before her career as an inventor, Brown worked as a home health aide. Her duties there inspired her camera inventions.

This early model of a closed circuit camera is a far cry from today's high tech models, but it was a breakthrough at the time.

patients at odd hours. Her husband, Albert, an electronics technician, worked more regular hours, and Marie was often home alone because of her varying shifts. She was thus particularly frightened when a rash of burglaries began occurring on her street. When she first became aware of the incidents, she considered adopting a guard dog, but after several dogs owned by a nearby business were shot during the course of a bungled burglary, she abandoned that idea.

To makes matters worse, police were often slow to arrive in **predominantly** black neighborhoods when they were called, and as crime rates skyrocketed across the city in the 1960s, the couple became determined to do something to combat the problem. The pair devised a system that featured a moving camera that could peer out of a series of peep holes. The images would then be transmitted to a closed circuit television (CCTV) for viewing. (Closed circuit systems are so-called because their signals are not publicly distributed but are instead monitored privately.) In 1966 they filed for a

patent, which was awarded three years later, on December 2, 1969. US Patent No. 3,482,037, which listed Marie's name as lead inventor, marked the first time closed circuit technology had been used for security purposes.

The system was considered so revolutionary that it was the subject of an admiring article in *The New York Times* on December 6, 1969. In the piece, reporter Stacey V. Jones informed readers that it could even be used from the com-

Brown's ideas of using cameras to watch over us has greatly expanded, with many cities blanketing their streets with surveillance.

fort and safety of a bedroom. She went on describe how homeowners could monitor the video and audio feed to see and speak to anyone seeking entry at the front door: If the visitor was welcome, he or she could be admitted into the home with a remote switch, or if there was an intruder, an alarm could be sounded. (The camera attached near the door was motorized so that it could scan up to view a tall person and down in the case of a child.)

Jones wrote, "Mrs. Brown pointed out the other day that it takes considerable time to dial the police and get action in an emergency. With the patented system a woman alone in the house could alarm the neighborhood immediately by pressing a button and installed in a doctor's office it might prevent holdups by drug addicts."

Some sources later reported that Marie won an award from a group called the National Scientists Committee, but aside from that and the small burst of publicity from *The New York Times*, the Browns received very little public attention. They reportedly sold the rights to their patent and barely profited from it.

Marie died in Queens on February 2, 1999. Her daughter, Norma, reportedly became a nurse and inventor; she is said to hold several patents on items aimed at improving home health care. ●

Words to Understand

aeronautical
having to do with airplanes and other flying machines

holography
a photographic technique that records the light scattered from an object
and then presents it in a way that appears three-dimensional.

Kenneth Dunkley

Anyone who has watched a movie wearing 3D glasses in the last few decades owes that experience in some part to Kenneth Dunkley, who in 1986 filed a patent for Three-Dimensional Viewing Glasses (3DVG). Dunkley's discovery that simply blocking two points in a person's peripheral vision would cause an ordinary 2D picture to appear in three dimensions—without the use of special lenses or mirrors—led to the glasses now distributed at theaters around the world.

Dunkley, who is of Jamaican and Trinidadian descent, was born in the New York City borough of Brooklyn, in 1939. He hails from a family of artists. His grandfather John Dunkley (1891–1947) is widely recognized as one of the most important Jamaican painters and sculptors of the last century, while his sister, Tina, and brother, Ernest, are both active in

Born:
1939

Nationality:
American

Achievements:
Inventor of the first
successful 3D glasses
used to watch film

the visual and performing arts. Assorted aunts, uncles, and cousins are also involved in various artistic endeavors.

By contrast, Dunkley, fascinated by the military planes that often flew over his childhood home during World War II, became an avid builder of model aircraft. He competed in the outdoor competitions that were then popular, vying with other local boys in such categories as "most beautiful model" and "fastest-flying model."

When the time came to choose a college, he decided to study **aeronautical** engineering and physics at New York University. After earning a B.S. degree, Dunkley completed the course work required for a doctorate, but never finished his thesis on the topic of holography. In 1973, during the course of his studies, however, he created the hologram "Thoughts," which gained widespread attention and is widely considered the first use of **holography** to produce an artwork.

During this period, Dunkley also found jobs as a seaman, instructor of physics at Brooklyn College, director of an afterschool science program, and holography consultant, among other work experiences.

In 1976, he joined the Princeton Applied Research Corporation, a global leader in the design and manufacture of instrumentation for scientific purposes, particularly in the field of electrochemistry, and he later worked as an optical systems specialist for Princeton Instrument Inc.

In the 1980s, Dunkley began giving a series of lectures at the Franklin Institute, a popular museum in Philadelphia. "The topic was holography and one of my points was

Dunkley's invention has led to several styles of 3D glasses.

a comparison of the 3D holographic image versus the flat 2D image from an ordinary photograph," he explained to an interviewer. "In 1985, during the course of examining the differences between monocular [one-eye] and binocular [two-eye] pinhole viewing of pictures under ordinary light, I accidentally positioned the pinholes off axis and observed what appeared to be a true stereoscopic 3D image. I called it the 3DVG effect."

Using that discovery, Dunkley fashioned his Three-Dimensional Viewing Glasses, which could take any ordinary picture in a magazine and turn it into a true 3D stereoscopic image. He applied for a patent in 1986 but was rejected on that and two other occasions. Finally, in 1989, he was granted the patent.

Dunkley now oversees his own Pennsylvania-based company, Holospace Laboratories. He has told journalists that he still gets thrilled when a naysayer sees for himself that 3DVG technology—which was the subject of a 1993 article in the highly respected scholarly journal published by the International Society for Optics and Photonics—actually works. "I never get over that. I love it," he has said. ●

Words to Understand

launch trajectories
the curved paths that launched objects follow to and from their destination

semiconductor
a material or object that allows some electricity or heat to move through it and that is used in electronic devices

spectrometer
an instrument used for measuring wavelengths of the light spectrum

thermomigration
a technique in which amounts of known impurities are made to migrate from the cool side of a wafer of pure semiconductor material to the hotter side when the wafer is heated

George Alcorn

Born:
1940

Nationality:
American

Achievements:
Inventor of X-ray
spectrometer; contributor to
many NASA space devices;
manager of space systems

Physicist George Alcorn, a respected pioneer in the field of **semiconductor** devices, holds eight patents—although the details of each are widely acknowledged to be just about impossible for a non-scientist to understand. One of his inventions, however, captured the imagination of the public despite its complexity: the imaging X-ray **spectrometer**, which helps researchers understand the composition of materials even when they cannot be broken down. Developed at NASA and patented in 1984, his device, as he has quipped, provided the space agency with "X-ray vision" and gave scientists a new way to try to find life on other planets.

Alcorn was born on March 22, 1940, to George Sr., who worked as an auto mechanic, and the former Arletta Dixon. The couple encouraged education, and both Alcorn

Alcorn began his scientific career by earning a degree in nuclear physics from the prestigious Howard University.

and his younger brother, Charles, took that advice to heart. Charles ultimately became a physicist and conducted research at IBM.

Alcorn, aware of the sacrifices his parents were making to help him attain a good education, became both a top student and skilled athlete at Occidental College, in Los Angeles, California, winning letters in baseball and football. He also earned his B.S. degree in physics in 1962, with honors.

"My father was always my idol," he told a reporter on the occasion of his 2015 induction into the National Inventors Hall of Fame. "I was impressed with his brilliance. He taught me that all obstacles in life could be overcome by hard work and determination."

Alcorn next studied at Howard University, earning a master's degree in nuclear physics in 1963. While studying for that advanced degree, he worked during the summers at North American Rockwell, a major aerospace company, for which he did computer analysis on the orbital mechanics and **launch trajectories** for various rockets and missiles. He was lucky enough to be involved with NASA's Titan and Saturn rockets, used on Apollo space missions—a big bonus for a young physicist.

Alcorn remained at Howard to earn his doctoral degree, completing his atomic and molecular physics studies in 1967. Upon earning his PhD, he began working for Philco-Ford. While it was a division of the Ford Motor Company, Philco-Ford also had an aerospace division, which developed satellite-tracking systems used by NASA's manned space program. He later signed on to work as a researcher for Perkin Elmer, a multinational technology company, and also did a stint as an advisor at IBM. Thanks to the relationships he forged at the latter company, in 1973 he was named an IBM Visiting Professor in Electrical Engineering at Howard and eventually became a full professor there.

Alcorn's work played a key role in many successful NASA rocket launches.

Alcorn joined NASA in 1978—a time when there were few African-American scientists at the agency—and it was there that he invented an imaging X-ray spectrometer that made pioneering use of the **thermomigration** of aluminum.

An X-ray spectrometer uses a focused beam of charged particles to excite X-rays in a sample. This lets researchers perform a detailed analysis of the material. It's especially useful for obtaining information about remote solar system and star-related objects. Alcorn's innovation involved developing a manufacturing process that used aluminum thermomigration. This allowed for a smaller, more sensitive device that revolutionized deep space exploration.

In 1984, Alcorn patented his device, which won him the title of NASA Inventor of the Year. He was promoted to the post of deputy project manager for the advanced development of new technologies for use on the International Space Station. In 1992, he became chief of the

This X-ray spectrometer, based on Alcorn's work, was part of a Mars rover mission.

Office of Commercial Programs for the Goddard Space Flight Center, where he was charged with finding ways space technology could be spun off for use in Earth-bound enterprises.

Alcorn, who retired from NASA in 2012, worked his way up in a variety of other leadership posts at the agency. At one point, he oversaw an experiment involving Robot Operated Material Processing Systems, which tested the possibilities for manufacturing material in the microgravity of space, and he also managed the Airborne Lidar Topographic Mapping System team, which made the first 3-D computerized maps of the nation's shorelines, forests, and other geographic features.

Alcorn's many laurels include NASA's Robert H. Goddard Award for Merit and Howard University's Heritage of Greatness Award. In addition to earning accolades for his research and discoveries, he has been widely recognized for his efforts to increase minority participation and diversity in the sciences. ●

George Alcorn:
Inventions that opened space

Lonnie Johnson

Many of the inventions in this book have created industries or made life simpler or easier for people. They involved science and engineering, or they provided a new way of doing something people had done for a long time. This inventor, however, came up with a new way for people to have a lot of fun. Along the way, he became a successful businessman and an inspiration to a generation of forward-thinking inventors.

Lonnie Johnson traveled a long road before becoming a multimillionaire toy developer. The third of six children, he was born on October 6, 1949, in Mobile, Alabama—the heart of the Jim Crow South. His father, David, a veteran of World War II, worked as a driver, and his mother, Arline, as a laundress and nurse's aide. During the summers, they both toiled picking cotton.

Born:
1949

Nationality:
American

Achievements:
NASA engineer; helped with numerous space missions; later invented popular toy; started aeronautics engineering company

Johnson, like many future engineers, enjoyed taking things apart to discover how they worked. He once took apart one of his sister's dolls, removing the head to study the mechanism that allowed its eyes to open and close. Because the family had little money to spare, Johnson sometimes made his own toys, including a device he fashioned from bamboo shoots that could propel pellet-like chinaberries. Once, he attached an old lawnmower engine to a cart built of scrap materials and zipped along a local road.

Because Mobile was a strictly **segregated** town, Johnson attended the all-black Williamson High School. Although he was an exceptionally gifted student, teachers there advised him to aim for a low-level career as a technician. Johnson remained undaunted by their warnings, however, pointing to the story of the **iconic** African-American inventor and scientist George Washington Carver as proof of the possibilities that might be open to him.

As a senior in 1968 Johnson represented Williamson High at the Alabama State Science Fair, held at the University of Alabama at Tuscaloosa. It was far from a welcoming place; just five years earlier, the state's racist governor, George Wallace, had attempted to prevent black students from enrolling there. Johnson was the only black student in the entire statewide competition. That didn't matter to the judges, apparently, as his entry—a robot built of scavenged material and powered by compressed air—took first place and a $250 cash prize.

When Johnson graduated from Williamson High in

The Oak Ridge National Laboratory complex in Tennessee gathers scientists from many disciplines to conduct key research.

1969, he won scholarships to Tuskegee University, the renowned, historically black school where Carver had once taught. At Tuskegee he earned a bachelor's degree in mechanical engineering in 1973 and a master's degree in nuclear engineering two years after that.

Upon leaving Tuskegee, Johnson worked as a researcher at the Oak Ridge National Laboratory, which is part of the U.S. Department of Energy. He later joined the US Air Force, and while in the military, served as an acting chief of the Space Nuclear Power Safety Section at a weapons lab in New Mexico. He was assigned to the Strategic Air Command (SAC) headquarters in Nebraska, and many sources credit him for his role in helping develop the stealth bomber program.

Johnson also worked at NASA's Jet Propulsion Laboratory in Pasadena, California, where he took on one of the most high-profile assignments of his career—working on the Galileo spacecraft. (Launched from the space shuttle *Atlantis* in 1989, Galileo arrived at Jupiter in 1995 and spent the next eight years circling that planet and sending back data.) Additionally, he served as an engineer during the early days of the Cassini spacecraft's mission to Saturn, a role that required him to ensure that no single systems failure would result in the loss of the entire craft.

While garnering numerous awards from the Air Force and NASA for his work on their behalf, Johnson was not content unless he was also engaged in his own projects. One of his ideas was to create a heat pump that would use water instead of the pollutant Freon. One day in 1982 he was testing a prototype in his bathroom, and when he pulled the lever, a powerful stream of water shot across the room into his bathtub.

Johnson had never lost the playful spirit that had inspired him to motorize a go-kart decades before. He immediately realized that he had stumbled upon a device that could make traditional squirt guns obsolete. After several years of tinkering to improve the design, he sold his idea to the Larami Corporation, which began mass-producing and marketing what they dubbed the Super Soaker in 1989.

The guns, which are currently made by the toy giant Hasbro, soon became one of the most popular toys in the world and have since generated an estimated $1 billion in sales.

Johnson, who was inducted into the State of Alabama Engineering Hall of Fame in 2011, now heads his own company. He holds some 100 patents, including those for an innovative ceramic battery and an automatic sprinkler system. Among the most far-reaching of his projects is the Johnson Ther-

Johnson continues his inventive and entrepreneurial work as leader of his own engineering firm.

moelectric Energy Converter (JTEC), a heat engine that can efficiently convert solar energy into electricity by splitting hydrogen atoms into protons and electrons. The JTEC, a self-contained unit that contains no moving parts, won the 2008 Breakthrough Award from the editors of *Popular Mechanics* magazine. While the technology is still being perfected, some experts feel it has the potential to transform the energy industry.

"Johnson will carve out a much greater place in history as one of the seminal figures of the ongoing green technology revolution," Paul Werbos, a former official at the National Science Foundation, has predicted. "This is a whole new family of technology....It's like discovering a new continent. You don't know what's there, but you sure want to explore it to find out." ●

Words to Understand

artisans
creative people who make useful things with their hands

bandwagon
in slang, it means people who become fans or supporters of something after it has become an established success

prototype
a model or example of a product being developed

Careers in Invention

There is no one set career path to becoming an inventor. Many inventors are engineers and scientists, but others have little or no formal education. While inventors as a whole don't share a common educational or work background, they do tend to share a mindset: passionate, curious, determined, bright, and action-oriented. Inventors generally thrive on solving problems and taking risks.

Many people who fit that profile are now becoming active in what is being called the "Maker Movement." When Benjamin Banneker was toiling by himself to hand-carve gears for his clock or Frederick McKinley Jones was trying to develop a refrigeration unit sturdy enough to withstand rough stretches of highway, they might never have conceived of such a thing.

"The Maker Movement is the umbrella

term for independent inventors, designers and tinkerers," an *Adweek* reporter wrote in 2014. "A convergence of computer hackers and traditional **artisans**, the niche is established enough to have its own magazine, *Make*, as well as hands-on Maker Faires that are catnip for DIYers who used to toil in solitude. Makers tap into an American admiration for self-reliance and combine that with open-source learning, contemporary design, and powerful personal technology like 3D printers."

Even the White House has gotten on the **bandwagon**. In 2014, President Barack Obama hosted a Maker Faire and put out a call to action that "every company, every college, every community, every citizen joins us as we lift up makers and builders and doers across the country."

However, since President George Washington signed off on the first patent in 1790 (to Samuel Hopkins for a process to make potash, an ingredient used in fertilizer), the road to creating and marketing a successful invention has never been easy. Some sources estimate that only a third of the applications at the US Patent and Trademark Office (USPTO) will be awarded a patent, and among those, only about five percent result in a commercial product.

Having an idea is only the first step. Successful inventors must ask themselves:

• Is the idea really new? (The USPTO maintains a searchable database of patents that have already been issued at patft.uspto.gov.)

• Is there actually a market for the product?

- Can it be developed and manufactured for a realistic cost and in a realistic time frame?

Aspiring inventors must be willing to build a **prototype** (not as daunting a prospect as in years past thanks to the availability of powerful software like Autodesk Inventor and affordable 3D printers); refine and troubleshoot the invention; file for the patent (a process for which many people hire a specially trained lawyer known as a patent attorney); and finally, manufacture and sell the invention.

The end of the invention? An official patent issued by the U.S. government.

It's never too early to start. Look at 11-year-old Frank Epperson, who in 1905 accidentally invented the Popsicle by leaving a cup of powdered fruit drink, water, and a stirring stick outside one cold night and years later, in 1923, obtained a patent for the frozen treat, or 16-year-old gymnast George Nissen, who created the first trampoline in 1930 by stretching material over a steel frame.

Today, we celebrate a national Kid Inventors Day, held each year on January 17, the birth date of Benjamin Franklin, who invented the world's first swim flippers at age 12. Its organizers advise that the best ways to celebrate are to: "Host an invention convention. Start a young inventors' club. Enter a contest. Keep an invention journal. Better yet, just design your own invention!" ●

Text-Dependent Questions

1. In what year did Benjamin Banneker publish his first almanac?

2. Why did sewing-machine needles leave scorch marks on fabric?

3. Why did Frederick McKinley Jones love the town of Hallock?

4. In what product were electret microphones first used?

5 At what popular Philadelphia museum did Kenneth Dunkley lecture?

6. How was George Alcorn's spectrometer different from those that had come before?

Suggested Research Projects

1. Look up how traffic lights have evolved and make a timeline of major innovations.

2. James West was the fourth African-American figure selected to join the National Inventors Hall of Fame. Who were the first three? Write a short paragraph on each of them.

3. Decide if you think consumers ate better before or after refrigerated trucks went into widespread use. Write a paragraph explaining your decision.

4. Tiny electret microphones can be purchased now for under a dollar apiece. Sketch an invention or product you might like to build using one.

5. Research project: *The New York Times* maintains an archive that dates back to 1851. Using the word "inventor" as a search term, find the oldest article you can and write a paragraph summarizing the article. Is the subject's invention still in use today?

6. Look for an image of Kenneth Dunkley's "Thoughts," which was the first use of holography to produce an artwork. What other holographic artworks can you discover? Write a short persuasive essay about whether or not you consider this type of art to be just as important as painting or sculpture.

7. Research the discoveries NASA has made using an X-ray spectrometer. Write a paragraph describing at least one you find interesting.

Find Out More

Websites

blackinventor.com/
The website of the Black Inventor Online Museum, which celebrates the ingenuity and accomplishments of black inventors throughout history.

teacher.scholastic.com/activities/bhistory/inventors/
A site maintained by Scholastic Publishers that includes profiles of several famed black inventors.

makezine.com/
A site devoted to the idea that every one of us can invent and make things. It includes projects, user forums, and more.

Books

Burker, Josh. *The Invent to Learn Guide to Fun*. Manchester, NH: Constructing Modern Knowledge Press, 2015.
The book features an assortment of classroom-tested "maker" projects that use LEGO blocks, old computers, and recycled materials.

Hackett, Chris. *Big Book of Maker Skills: 334 Tools & Techniques for Building Great Tech Projects*. New York: Simon & Schuster, 2014.
This is a tip-packed guide for taking your inventive projects to the next level—from basic wood- and metalworking skills to using power tools, from cutting-edge electronics play to 3D printing.

Maietta, Andrea, and Paolo Aliverti. *The Maker's Manual: A Practical Guide to the New Industrial Revolution*. N. Sebastopol, CA: Maker Media, 2015.
This is a practical and comprehensive guide with dozens of color images, techniques to transform your ideas into physical projects, and must-have skills like electronics prototyping, 3D printing, and programming.

Series Glossary of Key Terms

botany the study of plant biology

electron a negatively charged particle in an atom

genome all the DNA in an organism, including all the genes

nanometer a measurement of length that is one-billionth of a meter

nanotechnology manipulation of matter on an atomic or molecular scale

patent a set of exclusive rights granted to an inventor for a limited period of time in exchange for detailed public disclosure of an invention

periodic table the arrangement of all the known elements into a table based on increasing atomic number

protein large molecules in the body responsible for the structure and function of all the tissues in an organism

quantum mechanics the scientific principles that describe how matter on a small scale (such as atoms and electrons) behaves

segregated separated, in this case by race

ultraviolet a type of light, usually invisible, that can cause damage to the skin

Index

Photo credits

John Kropewnicki/DT 11; Lee Snider/DT 13; Carol Highsmith/LOC 14; Lasse Kristensen/DT 16; Biography.com 17; blackinventor.com 19; US Patent Office 20, 59; Gilles Paire/Dollar 22; Martin Lehmann/DT 24; Nitinut380/DT 26; tdoes/DollarPhoto 28; theroot.com 29; Oleg Zhukov/DollarPhoto 32; US Army 31; Gino Santa Maria/DollarPhoto 32; Brian Jackson/DollarPhoto 34; Jean Paul Chassenet/DT 36; Viappy/DollarPhoto 38; photographerlondon/DT 40; Koko2twins/DT 43; NASA/CXC/SAO 44; NASA/Goddard Space Flight Center 45; Josh Wash DC/Wiki 46; NASA 47; NASA/JPL-Caltech/Cornell/Max Planck Institut für Chemie/University of Guelph 48; Chris Hamilton 50; Oak Ridge National Laboratory/Department of Energy 53; Courtesy Johnson Battery Technologies 55; pathdoc/DollarPhoto 56.

About the Author

Mari Rich was educated at Lehman College, part of the public City University of New York. As a writer and editor, she has had many years of experience in the fields of university communications and reference publishing, most notably with the highly regarded periodical *Current Biography*, aimed at high school and college readers. She also edited and wrote for *World Authors, Leaders of the Information Age,* and *Nobel Laureates.* Currently, she spends much of her time writing about engineers and engineering.